Land beyond the Veil

Gladys Hargis

D1446011

Land Beyond the Veil
Copyrigh ©2016 by Gladys L. Hargis

ISBN-13: 978-1533645364

ISBN -10: 1533645361

Printed in the U.S.A.

In Memory

Twila June Stapel, my high school classmate,
and my beloved husband Warren R. Hargis

Foreword

There are many people who have thanked me for having the courage to write *You Live Forever* and this book, *Land Beyond the Veil*. I am not a writer, nor do I plan to be. If this had not actually happened to me, I would not be sitting here telling everyone about my experiences. I was given so much love from Mother Mary and the Holy Spirit, while spending many minutes in and out of Heaven, that I have not forgotten God's gift to me. I used some of my story from my first book, You Live Forever, to recap, for those who may not have read it, how I got to this part of my life, and was told by my spirits that I must share *all* of my story with you. God's spirits, always with you, will help lead you to salvation and prepare you for what is to come for all of us.

God gave you life, and He wants you to live it to the fullest, but He also wants you to love your neighbor as yourself and be kind to everybody.

Love is the only key to Paradise.

Gladys Hargis
2016

Contents

1

The Meeting Place

This is the second book that I have written, which you could probably say is a continuation of my first book, *You Live Forever* (published January 2011). Both of them begin with a miracle that happened August 5, 2006 when I was rushed to the hospital in Topeka, Kansas. I was nearly dead on arrival, then I finally did die at Stormont Vail Hospital. The paddles were used, I was brought back to breathing again. My blood pressure, I noted later from my medical records, was sometimes 20/5 and then 10/5. I was in and out of consciousness for days, in the Critical Care Unit.

Doctor Amir Arfaei became my lung doctor. After many tests, he and his team discovered my diaphragm was not responding, and I was not able to pump carbon dioxide out of my system; it was shutting my organs down. They ran all kinds of tubes down my throat, trying to find out what to do to keep me alive.

There were so many things that had happened to me that describing every miracle I was granted is hard to describe, like taking my first trip to heaven. To explain it all in detail is almost impossible. Since I was unconscious the biggest share of the time, my soul went in and out of my body. I was closer to death then I was to life. What I learned was that there are Angels with you long before your soul leaves your body. There is nothing to fear.

It was such a miracle to be able to actually die and see what God has made for our eternal life, beyond this life on earth. The stepping out of my body and watching doctors try frantically to get me to begin breathing again was another miracle. My heart doctor told me later that I looked like a pretzel, when he saw me in the emergency room. You would be surprised what they do to your body when desperation by emergency personal warrants it. All of their energy and attention goes into trying to bring you back to the land of the living.

This book will tell you some of the things that I left out of my first book, because I thought it was supposed to be my secret, and I did not want to share it with everyone. I soon realized that the pushing and the urging from unknown sources, which floated in and out of my mind, makes it impossible to keep it to myself.

2

Angels Appear

God sends many spiritual Angels down to help you, long before this stepping-out of the body occurs, and the heavenly spirits will be your guide for the rest of the trip to His kingdom and back—if you have been granted the miracle to return.

The Angels have their own agenda, and I just went along with their leadership. I saw them before my soul had left my body the first time. One was standing near the foot of my bed. When I heard the calling of my name, I saw the other Angel off to my side. The male Angel stayed with me the entire time, before I became unconscious, but more joined the young girl, who showed me the way out of my body, and to actually see them at that time was another miracle. This process was so easy and simple as there was no pain. I just rose and floated up.

I was able to stand to one side, and look down at my body. I was not standing on the floor, but was two to three feet above my body, watching what the doctors were doing to me. It was such a relief to rid myself of this shell of fat, tissue, bones and organs which holds my soul, and to be rid of this incumbency. Had I known it then, I would have understood more of what was going to happen to me, but I am getting ahead of my story and this time I will try to describe, more in detail of the miracles that wait to come to all of us.

God takes every opportunity that comes along, and He uses them as a lesson so that we humans can understand Him. I felt He was scratching the bottom of the barrel when He chose me because even though I loved Him dearly, I am just one of His flock and there were many more to choose from instead of me. So I just struggle along every day, waiting for instructions from Him who let me come back to this place called earth.

When I stepped out of my body again, I continued watching everything and looking down at the doctors, who were frantically trying to revive me. I saw the line go flat again, and nurses and interns putting on the paddles, to try and shock my body to keep it going. My heart beat was so slow, that it was hard to register at times. I saw them usher my husband and niece out of the room after asking them what possibly was wrong with me, and what symptoms had I been having before I was brought to the hospital. Warren said that I had been feeling terribly tired lately, but that was all he knew.

As I stood there watching, I never felt any sadness about walking off and leaving Warren, which seemed odd, as I loved him dearly, and I would not have wanted to ever leave him on his own, but it seemed natural for me just to walk away. I somehow knew that it was alright to go with the young Angel who had come after me. I had seen her minutes before, while I was talking to the doctor. I knew that this was what death was all about, and it was out of my control to do anything about it. Whatever was going to happen was going to happen, and it was in God's control, not mine.

3

Darkness and Hell

I walked behind the Angel, along the pathway, and over a bridge. Down below the bridge, I could hear painful mournful sounds of grief and sorry. There were large sewer holes that looked like the belly of a giant furnace belching out red hot coals. I understood at that moment that if you are evil and mean, and you have blackened your soul, that nothing in this world—or hell—will ever clean it back to being white and pure. Hell is just beyond our world, at the end of this life, and if you are doomed, you will never experience Heaven in all its glory.

I did not like the moans that I heard, nor did I want to stop and look, so I hurried after the Angel, who kept saying to me, "Hurry. Come with me, Gladys. You live forever, you live forever, you live forever, you never die... hurry, hurry." She did not want to stay here either, so I ran behind her, not letting her out of my sight.

4

Heavens' Doorway

I was being drawn upward, into this heavenly realm. I was able to experience the meeting of my personal Angel that led me up into another realm. After a few minutes, I passed through a white, brightly lit doorway, into the Land Beyond the Veil. That white doorway is the room that cleanses your soul and makes you pure with the wonderful *love* that wraps its arms around you. It cleans the very roots of your soul. When I stepped out of this room, I was dressed differently; my clothes were of fine material, and my dress came down around my knees. I had no shoes on my feet. I was as light as a feather, with energy of mass proportions. I was young again and agile. I could do anything I wanted. My eyes took in all my surroundings while I looked everywhere. You do not have tunnel vision in Heaven, so you can see almost everything at once.

5

The City of Heaven

The first thing I saw was the city that has been built for all of us to live someday. It was off in the distance, but I could see it, as it sparkled with brilliance and light. It looked like a prism of colors sparkling with a variety of colors, gold and silver, red and blues. The city had turrets, and buildings like Gothic descriptions; rounded edges, and soft corners. The background was blue and white, as if built on a hill, and sitting on a white cloud, running upward, toward the sky.

It looked like it was built in layers, with many miles of occupancy. It appeared to me to be built with the ground floor being the first layer then, as the ground and clouds got higher, so did the beautiful houses. Some buildings looked white as alabaster, with white portals and gazebo designs. There were porticos with green growth growing over the top and up the sides. Even though I was many miles away, I could see a lot of what the city looked like even from the vast distance.

I wondered if the more loving you had been on this earth, you earned a higher room in this mansion. God would live in the top floors, and I would be lucky just to earn a small space on the first floor.

I was so happy just to be there in the first place that I knew I was going to be very happy, so I did not care where I was placed.

6

My Brothers Meet

I remembered the incident, when my brother, Mark, died in 1990 in West Virginia. His wife, Norma, called and asked if we girls could come and see him one more time. He had lung cancer and wasn't expected to live much longer. We had to drive there, and I was afraid we would be too late. I let my sisters go and see him first, and then I saw him later that night.

As I walked in to his room, he was sitting on the edge of the bed. He was talking to someone in the room, but there was no one standing anywhere in the room. "He said he would hurry," he said even though he was talking to someone unseen.

He asked me if I saw my brother Lee, who had died five months earlier. I looked around, but I never saw him. Mark was insistent that Lee was standing at the foot of his bed. I said, "I thought that was nice that Lee came back to get you." Mark remarked that Lee had said, "Hurry, we have places to go and people to see." Mark said to me, "How can I hurry any faster?" I told him that God would take him when it is time.

Mark left us later that night. Lee was impatient, but I hoped he had waited. We have things to do up there in that land, we have places to go and people to see. What fun we will all have.

When I saw the city, I remembered this incident, and had gained the knowledge that we would not just lay around doing nothing.

It is exciting to know that surprises are yet to come for all of us.

7

Heavenly Meeting Place

As I looked around, I noticed waves of grasses stretching over vast areas and small hills. They seemed alive, as if waving in welcome. It reminded me of the Flint Hills in Kansas. Then I was reminded by the Angel who was standing next to me, to come with her. I wanted to continue to look around some more. It was so beautiful, and I had to drag my eyes away, but she seemed to want me to continue to go with her instead.

Standing next to me was another Angel, and she told me it was time to go with her as well. I did not know what they had in store for me, but this one took me over to four other Angels who were standing in a group.

I asked if I could go back and get Warren, my husband of many years, as I wanted him to see this beautiful sight. I had shared such a long life with him and I hated to leave him behind to fend for himself. This was such a surprise question to the four Angels because they started talking to each other and seemed surprised at my request. They turned around, so I could not hear their conversations. They seemed to ignore me for quite some time. I could not hear them talking with their backs to me. I finally understood, that when they talk to each other, they talk with their mind. It is only when they turn back to you and open their minds up, that they let you hear their thoughts.

21

8

My Husband's Mother

I finally ignored them and continued looking around at such beauty, when I noticed a Veil hanging down between me and a beautiful garden. The Veil was clear enough to see the outlines of people moving about, but it was not as clear as I would have liked it to be. The Veil was cut like a steeple on a church steeple, closed at the top and open at the bottom.

First I hesitated about leaving the Angels, but they did not seem to care where I went. When no one was answering my question, I inquired if I could see my mother and father. Again no one seemed to answer me. Then I asked if I could see Warren's mother, and I heard a voice beyond the veil say, "Thank you for the ball and the cross". It was clearly a woman's voice, but I did not know who it was, or why I was told this. I was to learn later on. The answer to this was another miracle that I write about in more detail in Chapter 17.

Land Beyond the Veil / Gladys Hargis

9

Meeting My Dad

I continued walking through the Veil. On the path that led into the Garden—when outside the gate—at the corner of the Garden was a middle age man standing with his booted foot resting on the stone corner post. He acted like he knew me, and he grinned and called me by my name, "Gladys." Then he said, "Sis, this is not your time to come here yet. You have another job to do, and you must go back."

I wondered how he knew that I had a job to do, but when he called me "Sis" I then knew who he was. My father had so many daughters in his family that he called all of us "Sis", as he knew someone would answer.

He was dressed in what looked like a silk riding shirt, with pants that stopped just below the knees. His riding boots were of excellent leather, and they came up to his knees. The clothes he wore looked expensive. He said that God had other plans in store for me, and that he himself would see me again soon. He then turned to leave, going down the sidewalk and into a large gray building. The building looked like it had two-foot thick walls, with windows that had no screens. Later, when I told my husband, Warren, he said he guessed that there were not any heavenly flies there. My dad stopped and turned back to me and waved, and said again that he would see me soon.

He turned away from me and was gone. I realized that walking through this building was the way to get into the city proper. It was surprising why I knew that at the time, but yet I did. Some things I saw were familiar to me, as if I had been there at a different time in my life, and yet some things I saw were a complete surprise.

I looked back to see if the Angels had come to a decision yet, about my going back to get Warren, but they were still in group session, so I turned and continued on to the path that led into the Garden.

10

My Mother in the Garden

There were three people softly yelling and motioning for me to come and see them. I hurried along, but when I finally reached the gates, they had disappeared. As I continued walking on, and getting deeper into this beautiful place, I noticed a brightly lit area off to my right. It looked interesting and I was curious, but I did not think I had enough time to check everything out, so I continued on my way.

I was starting to notice the flowers all around me and the beautiful aroma that the flowers were giving out. They seemed to beg me to touch them and enjoy their beauty. They were all different colors, succulent, wet, flowers of all kinds, some that I knew and some colors that I had never seen before. Some were pastels and some were dark. Some had moisture oozing from them, as if they were telling you that they had just been rained on. Their wet consistency sparkled and shone, almost like they were alive and well. They all seemed to be able to sing in harmony, they appeared perfect, and they did not have thorns.

The roses were all colors, peonies, tulips, lilacs, lilies, and on and on, almost beyond your imagination. Trees of majestic proportions and heights towered upward. But I never saw animals of any kind. I did see some doves sitting in a tree, singing their songs.

I saw my mother walking up through the Garden, carrying a, three-year-old girl. Even though I had been born long after

27

Emma Margaret died at three weeks, I knew it was her. She looked like my oldest sister Mary Grace.

Emma Margaret had on a dress of red velvet, which did not have any seams that I could see. That left me with wonderment. How did these heavenly people get their clothes onto their bodies? Were they glued on, painted on, or did they use Velcro, and somehow hide the seams?

Walking along beside my mother was my brother Carroll, who had died at the age of seven of an appendix that burst, before my parents could get medical help. My older brothers, Lee and Mark, had died just fifteen years earlier than my visit to the Garden, and they were there as well.

When I reached my mother, she was smiling and seemed happy to see me, but she also told me that this was not my time to be with her. I was to go back. I wanted to ask her why my dad was not with her and my siblings, but in my mind's eye I realized that my dad really belonged to his first wife Brooke, and their children. At the time it seemed alright, and maybe God would be able to explain it to me in time.

After I spent some time talking to everyone, my mother told me it was time for me to go back. Again I wondered how she knew I was to return to do a job for God.

I turned and walked back up the lane, toward the pathway to the opening of the Veil, but before I went through, I took another path. I seemed to have plenty of time and I wanted to see the very bright lighted area that was off to the left and ahead of me.

When I arrived, I could see large alabaster pillars standing by themselves, rising high into the sky. It appeared as if the sun was high above my head, and there was no shaded area anywhere around me, yet to my left, and further away from the lighted area, were large alabaster pillars holding up two-by-six cross-beams spaced to let in the light. Green ivy vines were woven through them to let in the light, and yet to shut out the brightness of the light. Young maidens were enjoying a small stream.

11

Saint Theresa

To, my right, I saw a young girl dangling her bare feet back and forth, sitting on a cement garden bench, leaning forward, with her hands bracing herself. She was smiling with so much love. She called out and introduced herself as Saint Theresa, like I was supposed to know her, but I did not, so I just smiled back. Had she been there for a purpose, or just by accident? There were so many questions that left me to wonder why I should know her.

I learned later that Catholics hold Saint Theresa in reverence, as their patron saint. I am not Catholic, so I did not know. I had time to study her while wondering how she knew she had been chosen to be a saint. Were we, I wondered, all assigned a job and given a title?

But, why would she make it a point to see me? What connection would I have with her? The mysteries were mounting.

I would have to wait and see what was in store for me.

Saint Theresa was sitting near a bed of roses of all shades. The scent that was coming from, and glistening off of, the roses was overwhelming. The flowers seemed to be alive, almost singing among themselves. Water seemed to seep out from the leaves.

I acknowledged the Saint, but I never did understand who she was, and she was sitting in that spot, as if she did not want to miss my approach or miss seeing me.

Maybe someday I will learn the answer.

12

Mary, the Mother of Jesus

As I got closer to the bright light, I glanced to my left and saw a woman who looked so beautiful. She was dressed like a queen. She was sitting in a comfortable chair, with grace and leisure. You could tell the alabaster white chair was molded to fit her body. She looked like royalty, with a small crown on her head. Her hair was coiled and piled upon her head. It looked like her hair had been done up just to hold her crown in place, yet it looked like it would have stayed in place anyway.

Her gown reached the ground. Its colors were pastel, wine and blue. The jewels around her neck were of diamonds and pearls. Her veil was worn around the back of her head and down over her shoulders and then wrapped around her arms, as if hugging her. She had a long ringlet coiled and hanging down outside of her veil that covered her head, under the crown. It, was the only curl I saw, but it seemed so natural to me to see her hair like this. , I knew who she was within an instant, and it took my breath away.

Here was my beloved Mary, the mother of my Jesus. I was so overwhelmed with love that I bowed and dropped to my knees, and then I lay prostrate on the ground, at her feet. She then smiled and touched me to rise and sit near her on the garden seat.

My seat was also alabaster which, after I set down, molded to my body. She gave me time to take in my surroundings, and then she would asked me a lot of questions.

There were four majestic looking Angels standing near her, in reverence yet on guard. Three of them were standing quite close, the older one was behind her and further away. They had on long rich-looking robes, with roped belts around their waists, hanging down almost to their hems. One held a staff and one held a spear. The older two had wings that were mostly hidden among the material of their clothes.

The third one was just standing there watching everything that was going on. The fourth one was younger. He looked about fourteen and held a small book that was trimmed in gold. He didn't seem to be reading from it, but it was open in his hand. He would glance at it from time to time and, in a low voice, he would answer Mary when she asked him a question. You could tell the way they stood near her they were there to reverently help her. You could see they loved her very much, by the looks in their eyes.

After she let me finish looking around, she asked me how my life had been, growing up with my Mother and Father? Whom had I married and if I had been happy? I instantly knew she already knew the answers, but she seemed to be putting me at ease, just by asking me the questions. We talked for a long, long time, it seemed like many, many, hours. I had no thought of hurrying back to the gate of the garden. I knew I wanted to spend all my time with this beautiful woman. I felt I had finally come home.

The longer we talked, I knew that I shared a common bond with her in some way; a relationship with her that I could not understand. I had hoped that Mary might tell me what connection we had, but when I asked she just smiled and said she would tell me when it was time. She did tell me I was of her family, but I thought she meant her heavenly family.

She spent quite a bit of time talking about my marriage. She knew that I wanted to go back and get Warren so he could be with me, and see this beautiful place. Warren had been so good to me, and he too loved God. It seemed so natural to talk one-on-one with her. I wanted Warren to share this time with me. I told Mary that we had talked about wanting to come together to Heaven, but if that was not possible, then I would like to go back and help prepare him for this journey.

He was getting old and he was having a hard time walking. He had fallen several times while working for the Fire Department and, after he had retired, he accidentally had fallen nine feet out of a garage loft, hitting his head on the cement floor and knocking himself out for over three hours, causing him to break his collarbone and ribs. All of his Doctors told him that he should have been killed, but that someone was watching over him from Heaven.

He was such a wonderful person and he loved God so much and had always tried to keep his commandments. I just did not think he deserved such a fate to have to struggle through the rest of his life on earth without me to help him. I had presented my request to Mary, but she just smiled and said that in time I would be told.

In Heaven you don't get your answers right away. This is where your patience comes into play, and your faith in God plays a big part of your life. Only He knows the answers.

We continued talking for what seemed like many hours, about many things. It seemed like we went on forever, yet, since there is no time in heaven, it seemed as if it was only a short time. It was only much later that I realized I had been in and out of my body many times over the past twenty-one days, so that most of my time had been spent with her.

This wonderful woman, Mary, said that I was to be blessed and made holy. She also said again that I was of her family, I felt like she was trying to tell me something important, but again I asked her what that meant, and she just smiled and said I would know in time.

She also said I was to rule. What she meant by this, she would not say. I asked her if we were talking about when I went back to earth, but she said no, it would be later when I returned

33

to Heaven. I laughed and ask if it was going to be like Queen Elizabeth, and she just smiled and said, "Much higher." She said I had royal blood in my veins, which did not surprise me, as my mother had told me that royal blood was from the English illegitimate side. My sister and I could never find the connection to this. We knew that other family members may have made the connection, but we could not find that information for ourselves. I would have to find out what Mary meant when she was ready to tell me.

I did not want to end the visit with this wonderful Mary. I knew that she was going to be my friend and confident for the rest of my time, if I was to go back or stay. I wanted so badly for Warren to meet her. She was the kind of person whose love was natural and truthful. She was my mother, my sister, my friend, all wrapped up in one package. She had four wonderful angelic Angels standing guard over her, surrounding her, at her beck and call. She had a band of Angels singing her praises, and I was to share in this beautiful chorus and be privileged to be called into her presence. What a wonderful honor that I had with her.

I asked her if we were born many times, or on loan from Heaven. She seemed surprised by the question, and inquired why I had asked. I told her that I had a recurring dream of a young child who had olive skin and almond eyes, and when I was certain it was me, I wondered why I looked so different now. She smiled and said that those questions would also be answered in time. I was originally a blond, blue-eyed girl. I have had that same dream since I was quite young. In my dream, I was about 9 years old, and then everything ceased to be. Where did I go? Why was I here? When would I understand?

She talked to me like a friend of long-standing, as if I had known her all my life, and I guess I had. We talked of old times, and what I had done to fulfill my life. We talked of the privileges I had been given and what I had done with my time on earth. Then she told me that I was to continue with my life and I

34

would be sent back to do another job for her. She said that she would guide me and share with me the answers that I would need to continue with my job on earth. She told me I was only loaned out., that my time from now until I returned was only temporary. She assured me that my love for Warren was outstanding and that most people did not have this opportunity to find a husband that was so kind and loving.

She told me that I was to be honored and glorified, and I was to go back and help my husband to get ready for Paradise. She also told me that I was to share all the love that she had bestowed on me with, everyone I saw. I was to tell the world about this heavenly place and give people hope.

This love that Mary bestowed upon me is so overwhelming that it seeps out of every pore of my body. It circles me like a shroud, as it is with me and will never leave me. She said she would send with me the Angels who would guide me and watch over me until I returned. There would be things that I would know later, and I knew Mary had granted me my wish, to go back and help Warren with his struggles.

I did not want to leave her, but I finally turned and walked away, and this Blessed Mary assured me that I would return in a short time after Warren left earth. She said the Angels she was sending back with me would call my name and tell me when it was time to follow her instructions. They would watch over me, she said, and keep me safe.

13

Entering Earth's Gates

W hen I got back up to the doorway to the garden, I was met by the group of Angels who had been talking about my going back. They told me that it had been decided that I would return to earth. They also made it clear that I had a job to do, and then I would return to Heaven.

I was led out to a doorway that was small, and a Veil was clearly across it. There seemed to be several doorways that I had to go through, but I was not afraid because I was guided by a Holy Spirit. Then I saw a dark area, and realized that the Spirit was still with me. She told me not to be afraid,"… as we will always be with you until you return."

Mary had said that the Angels she was sending back with me would call my name and tell me when it was time. I have heard my name called several times since I have returned, but usually it is heard as a thought, and speaks of a job for me to do.

I learned, while in Heaven, that you communicate with your thoughts. Sometimes I can hear the Angels thoughts, and other times they shut me off. Their language is universal and you can understand what is said—if they let you hear them. It reminds me of someone outside the door, you can hear murmurs, but you cannot understand what is being said.

Now I feel their presence every day and know they are around me. I was given the gift of awareness to God's miracles.

14

Brought Back to Life

Since I was declared dead in the hospital, I was brought back to life several times. I was put into critical care and watched very closely for eight days. I was unconscious for many days, yet I would sing hymns, all the verses. I would call my sister even though I was unconscious, and I could talk to her. After laying down the phone, the nurses knew I was still unconscious, and I could not remember calling my sister after I awoke. Strange things happen to you while you are in that state.

Dr. Arfaei, my lung doctor, could not explain it. He said later that he knew my soul had left my body several times; he could feel another being behind him. I told him that I witnessed him putting a tape recorder under my pillow one night while I was standing behind him, and he looked at me shaking his head, with tears coming out of his eyes.

When I awoke, Dr. Arfaei had decided I was not going to live. My blood pressure was still around 20/5, and breathing was barely noticeable. I was finally put into the hospice section, to wait for the Angel of Death to come for me. When, after many days, I awoke, a pretty nurse by the name of Rose sat on the foot of my bed.

She kept saying to me, "Let your soul leave your body, Gladys.". I thought she was Mary, whom I had just been talking to, and when I asked her if she was Mary, she smiled and said "No." Then I asked if she was Saint Theresa, and she just smiled and shook her head. She still continued telling me to let my soul leave my body. I could not understand what she was telling me, as the Angel had told me I could stay, and Mary had said I could stay. I told Rose that and she shook her head.

I could see Warren standing in the partially open doorway, waiting to come into my room.

Beside my bed, stood a female Angel who appeared to be middle-aged, wearing a flowered design dress, waiting to take me up to Heaven with her. I told the Angel that Mary told me I was to stay to take care of Warren and to do a job for her. I asked Rose who that woman was standing near her, and she answered, "Yes, I have seen her before. She is waiting for you, so let your soul leave your body."

I knew we were in a stand-off. I was not planning to go anywhere and, finally, the Angel walked besides my bed. I wanted to touch her, but my body had been medically manipulated so badly when I was brought into the emergency room, that I could not straighten out my arms. The middle-aged Angel walked out of my hospice room, through the wall behind my bed. Warren told me later that he had seen a male Angel who had followed her out as well. Warren was so amazed to have witnessed this and been a part of God's wonders.

After the Angels left, a few days passed and I seemed to be improved. The nurses noticed that I was more alert and talkative. My blood pressure was climbing higher, and it was decided that I might be going to live after all. Rose, my nurse, told Doctor Arfaei about the Angels appearing and then their leaving my bedside. The doctor saw it was a sign to put me back on oxygen and air.

They took some more tests and, after being examined by many doctors that paraded in and out, I was taken out of the hospice section and put into a private room. My brain function had been at the very edge of life as I knew it. My being out of hospice was another miracle.

I can remember the building blocks of my brain tumbling back and forth and up and down, re-shuffling, to bring my brain back to the understanding of what was going on around me. This in its self was an amazing miracle, to be able to watch it from the inside out and to see GOD's workmanship, allowing me to understand all of what was going to happen to me again.

My learning ability had opened up again, God was granting me renewed energy and the ability to think. I had been to Paradise, saw Mary, her Angels, the City, the Garden, my mother and father, brothers, and sister—what a wonderful miracle this had been for me. I still remember this wonderful event. No wonder I hold everything near and dear to my heart.

The love that was given to me at that time was—and still is— so overwhelming that there is no way to explain it. I will never in my lifetime ever be able to explain what I saw in this wonderful place called Heaven.

Dr. Arfaei told me that I would never be able to lay down flat without oxygen and air coming into my lungs. My diaphragm seemed to be paralyzed and would not expand. I am not able to expel the carbon dioxide in my lung and passages. My left lung was too small and could have been stymied by exposure to asbestos/ or a foreign chemical. I was told that if I ever went to sleep longer than two hours without this equipment, my organs would shut down and I would die within a short time.

After many more days in the hospital, I was encouraged to try to walk. I had been down more than twenty-one days, so it was painful to use my legs. I had to drag an oxygen and air tank along as well. After I was able to accomplish this, and get back upon my feet, I was transferred to the Rehab Hospital for eleven more days. I was finally sent home with a walker to aide me.

Land Beyond the Veil / Gladys Hargis

15

Jobs To Do For Mary

I guess I thought that the angelic Angels would be there to welcome me home, but I saw and heard nothing. Yet I knew that what I had experienced was real, and I would have to just bide my time. Mary would send me Angelic Spirits soon enough, and I would just have to wait.

The first couple of nights, I rested and was getting use to my pump and air pack running at night. Warren asked if I would get my feelings hurt if he slept in the spare bedroom. He said the squeal of the oxygen pump was so noisy that it disturbed his rest. I told him that was understandable and for him to go ahead and make the change. Besides, his cat usually walked across my air pack machine and shut it off accidently, so everything worked out for the best.

I had two weeks of good rest and recovery, but I was always listening for the voices to call my name. In the daytime I would write down what I remembered, in case I might forget. Now, ten years later, I still remember everything I saw when I visited that wonderful place, and the Garden of Heaven. I know I will never forget any of it because God and Mary are here to remind me.

I still did not know what I was to do. I kept looking for the printing on my walls, in big blocked letters, telling me what I am supposed to be doing for Mary. I waited for a miracle to appear with the answer.

One night, I again heard a voice call my name, telling me to write it all down so as not to forget. I could not believe that Mary would give me this chore. I am not a writer. But she seemed to have faith in me, even though I did not have faith in myself. I did it wrong at the beginning when I printed large chapters I and 2, and then I realized that I could not send the material out to be published like that, so I cut a lot out and trimmed it down, so as to not have it too long to read. Then I almost took out too much.

I was getting frustrated with the Angels who were around me, and accused them of leading me down a dark pathway, that even they did not seem to understand either. I was way out of my depth and drowning. I did not like where this book was heading. I never forgot anything I wanted to say, I just did not know how to say it. So I gave it up for over two weeks.

I finally had some peace until one night I woke up in the middle of the night with a bumping of my bed. Not just one bump, but many bumps. I could also feel someone sitting on my bed. I thought my husband was coming in to sleep with me and, in the dark, he could not find the bed, and had bumped into it. I turned on my light to make it easier for him, but there was no one in my room. I went in to check on him, but he was sound asleep.

I was stymied, but I finally had everything written down in book form. I always felt that the Angel, Mary had promised me, was around somewhere. The Spirit usually did not let me forget it. I did realize then that no one else on earth could see my Spirits. The Angels did not come here to be gazed upon. I cannot see anyone else's, either, but I am very much aware of them.

After I polished my book off, retyped it two or three times, I then found a publisher, which I know now was another mistake. I have made lots of mistakes. I did not want to tell everyone, everything I saw. I felt that some of the things that Mary told me were mine, which I hold near and dear to my heart. Now I

44

realize that, at the Spirits urging, I am to share it all with everyone. Sometimes I clench my teeth and refuse to tell all, but I usually give it up in the end. This Spirit is stronger than I am.

My book was published January, 2011. It sold quite well, both through the publisher and out of my home.

16

Warren's Angels

That year with Warren was being used up with the sale of the books and, even though we spent a lot of time together, time was starting to slip by. After it was on the market, I never heard any more voices from the Heavenly Spirit about my book, but I was aware that Warren and I were not alone.

In January, just one year before Warren passed away, he came into my room and told me that he could hear someone talking outside his window. He always slept with the windows down tightly and would not let fresh air into his room at night. He was never afraid, but he did not like the voices..

At first I did not hear the voices then, and after listening carefully, I was starting to hear them as well. I could never find out where the voices were coming from until one evening I saw a shadow moving away from the house. Who or what it was, I could only guess.

I had seen the shadows before. I could not understand them, nor could I see them clearly, but I wondered if they might be there for Warren. When I told him that they meant no harm, he was okay by that and seemed to be at peace.

Warren did ask one night if they would be coming after him, and I assured him that the Angelic Spirits would probably be around until we both left to make the journey to the Land Beyond the Veil. I told Warren that we would have to continue

47

living our lives with them, as we were nearing the end of our life on this earth, and we both would be called to come home.

I prayed silently that it would be together.

17

Ball and Cross Miracle

In 1993, Warren and I had helped to clean out his grandparent's house in Holton, Kansas, a town just north of our home in Topeka, when I came across some letters from Warren's mother. I had put them away in my filing cabinet and kept them with the intention of reading them at a later date. Warren and I forgot all about them.

After I'd had the near death experiences, we thought we should get our house in order also and throw away things we did not need. We came across Esther's letters, which were dated January 5, 1929, just six months before she was killed. When I was in Heaven, I asked if I could see Warren's mother, Esther. The voice who answered me beyond the Veil, thanked me for the "ball and the cross". In the letter, Esther thanked her mother and sisters for the beautiful gold cross she had been given for Christmas that year.

On July 15, 1929, Warren's mother was accidently killed along with her about-to-be-born baby daughter, Emma Ruth. When I asked Warren's Aunt Julia Hargis, at a 2007 family reunion, what she remembered about the funeral of Warren's mother that might involve him seeing his mother lying in the casket.

Warren was barely two in 1929. Aunt Julia said that she was holding Warren and, when he looked down and saw his mother laying in the casket, he reached for her, dropping the little red rubber ball he had been holding, in the casket.

Julie remembered saying to Warren, "Oh look, honey, you gave your mother a gift." Aunt Julie did not want to rummage around in the casket to get the ball back, so she just walked away. She remarked that Esther had been wearing a beautiful little gold cross.

Aunt Julie had always lived in Missouri, and Warren had never heard about what had happened the day of the funeral. No one ever talked about it. It had been a terrible tragedy. I met Warren for the first time in 1948. I would never have known about Esther Kuglin Hargis's death, or even heard about it in any way. So how did I know about it while in an unconscious state?

The relatives never talked about this tragedy.

This, to me, was further proof that I had been to Heaven.

18

The Slippery Slope

Warren now realized that his health was in decline, as he had two more bouts with dreadful kidney stones, and then he started getting bladder and leakage infections.

Warren was in the hospital with more stones when Dr. Arfaei came running into the emergency room. Dr. David Kingfisher was right behind him, and said "What's going on?" Dr. Arfaei then saw me sitting nearby. Jumping into my lap and kissing the top of my head, he said to me, "You are my Angel. Because of you, I am going to be a better man. I love you Gladys." Then he leaped off my lap and left the room. All Doctor Kingfisher could say was, "Good grief" as he, too, left.

Warren asked who that doctor was, and wanted to know why had he hugged me. I told Warren that Dr. Arfaei knew I had seen an Angel, and he had witnessed my soul leaving my body. When I said that, Warren laughed through the pain.

Warren tried to help me realize that sometime in the future I was going to have to get along without him. I had already been told this, but it was still going to be hard to accept. Every day I asked God for more time. I would say, "Just let me have another two years" then I asked for one more year, but I knew that time was running out for us. We were both ready, but I wanted to go with him when he left this earth. I was sorry I had asked to close out my life, which meant I would have to stay for a while to get things in order so that my son and daughter-in-law would not have so much to deal with.

Warren had neuropathy of his legs, which meant his brain and his legs did not work together. He could not feel his legs at times. If he was sitting down and he crossed them, then he would get up to walk and forget to uncross them, and fall.

I hated it when I had to take his car keys away from him. His eyes were failing him, where he could not see the difference between the curbing and the street, and he would drive over the sidewalk. Finally, he agreed that it was time to let me drive him around.

My back had been injured at my last place of employment, years before, but I wore a back-belt which helped me help him, get back up whenever he fell. He could use his strength in his arms, but his legs were not manageable, so he needed whatever help I could give him. He refused to walk with a walker when he was out in public. I conceded to give him this last wish. My children would help him by taking his arms and, when he would step off the sidewalk, he would start running. They would all laugh and say, "Whoa, Dad, we got you." He would laugh and Tammy, our daughter-in-law, would catch him. He always had a good sense of humor, and he would just laugh at his own antics.

One night, six months before Warren left us with his Angels, he came into my bedroom and said he could not sleep. It was about 1:30 AM. Going to sleep was never a problem with him, but it was that night. We both sat and looked out the window.

There was a moon out, and we could see a light mist swirling around the neighbor's yard. Suddenly, Warren gasped and called my attention to voices of two small children laughing. He then said he saw a woman walking about three feet off the ground. She was dressed in a long gown of blue and wine, which billowed out, like a hoop, and a light, thin veil hanging down from her neck, around her back and around the children at her side. The Children were playing peek-a-boo with each other, around their mother's skirts.

52

They were walking across the back yard. The children had blond hair, the mother's hair was dark and hung below her neck line. He could see the faces of the children, but he could not see the mother's face. She just disappeared into the fog around her.

Warren wondered aloud if she was his Mother. I somehow knew that it was, so I told him yes. I did not tell him that I could not see them quite as plainly as he did, but I knew it was a sign, and I felt they were here for him. The next day, he said that he was happy to see such a sight, and he knew he was given a gift to see what was to come for all of us.

Only once in a while would either he or I hear what sounded like voices, but they were elusive and far away; Spirits coming and going nearby. Warren was more aware of them now and he felt more at peace. He knew they were here for everyone, and not just us.

In late October 2012, he started having trouble with his stomach. When it was too hard for me to support his walking, we started eating out for breakfast, at a local drive-in. After a couple of weeks, he awoke one morning and said it felt like he has just eaten a nine course meal. I knew we had to see the doctor to find out why he was so full all the time.

After many tests of his colon, the cancer doctor was called in. His blood work was done and it found Asbestos/Mesothelioma Cancer. It had grown so fast, and had wrapped around his stomach and esophagus, shutting everything off. When the doctor told Warren that he had bad news, a large tear came from his eyes. I told him that he could go to hospice or come home, which did he want to do? He said he wanted to come home. I was happy for that, as I knew that Mary would give me strength to get through this, and her Angelic Spirits would help me as well.

We brought him home with the assistance of Midland Hospice, who helped me tend to him. A neighbor girl wanted to help and Warren's cousin, Elizabeth, who was a surgery assistant at St. Francis Hospital, came to stay with me, too. He lived eighteen days, days we spent talking. He tried to prepare me on how to carry on alone. He promised that he would meet me by the Gate.

I had been with him until late when I could feel a presence in the room. I kissed him on the forehead and told him I loved him. He had family by his side. After the children went to bed his Angel came for him.

He died November 24, 2012. I miss him every day, but I know he is in good hands, and is at peace with his Lord.

19

Unknown Spirit

I n 2014, I was coming back from a trip down town when I saw a shadow crossing the road near my car. At first I thought it was a reflection of a car passing by, but then I realized that it was a figure of a man walking quite fast. He was more transparent then solid, and then he just dissolved into nothing.

When I got home, I told Elizabeth, Warren's cousin who had been living with us and stayed on after his passing. She was in the living room, reading, and I asked her if she ever sees anything like the shadow of the man I described. I told her that he was short, probably about five foot, but no more. Elizabeth said that she had seen a figure answering that description out of corner of her eyes, but not in the house; he was outside and she had only seen him in shadows. She hadn't mentioned it to me before because she was waiting to see if I would acknowledge him.

I had not seen the man clearly, but I have come to realize that everyone has their own spirits. I cannot see yours, and you cannot see mine. They are not to be looked upon, nor admired; they are here to do a job for the Lord. If you ask God for help, you are assigned a Holy Spirit, then only you will be in accordance with them. Only you will see them.

I am sure that there are many of these spirits out and about, handling everybody's business. They all have their own agenda and many jobs are assigned to them.

Many know the spirits exist, but some of them have been taught that they are evil and belong to Satan. I know, from the miracles that I have witnessed, that is not true. When I ask people I know if they have ever seen a spirit, They will often give me a big smile as they respond with a resounding, "Yes. I know they are nearby. I can feel their presence".

In April of 2014, I became even more aware of them. My lung doctor had just told me that I was to never lie down in bed without putting on my air and oxygen mask. My diaphragm was paralyzed and would not respond, it could no longer push out the carbon dioxide that I breathed in. I was told that if I fell asleep without my oxygen mask, I had only a two-hour leeway and my organs would start shutting down. I would die if the problem was not recognized within that time period.

Elizabeth was gone for the day. I laid down for a short afternoon nap. I had been having trouble with my jaw, a painful bout of TMJ, or painful jaw spasm. I had taken a muscle relaxer to ease the pain. I forgot to read the dosage on the bottle— which instructed me to cut the pill in half. I naturally took a whole one—twice the recommended dosage.

I laid down on my bed without the mask. I only meant to rest a while, but I fell into a deep sleep. No more than ten minutes went by when a forceful blast of hot air came down from the corner of my bedroom where there were no vents or registers. The furnace had been shut off in anticipation of a workman coming out to clean it the next day. Besides, the weather was warm, so we did not need it.

The blast woke me up immediately. Coming out of a sound sleep, I was confused and got up to see if Elizabeth had come home. When I saw that I was alone, I dismissed the blast of heat as a figment of my imagination. I laid back down, once again forgetting to put on my mask. And again another even harder blast of very hot air came down, right into my face. Startled awake, I could hear the air as if it were being blown by something or someone very powerful. It had come from the same corner of my bedroom ceiling as the first blast. This time it hit me with a shock that someone or something had just saved my life. I realized I had put my life in jeopardy by not having on the mask, and I was being told to put it on.

After adjusting my mask, I thanked God for his kindness and I lay back down to sleep. I slept for over six hours. I would have been dead if I had not received this gift from my Angelic Spirits.

Land Beyond the Veil / Gladys Hargis

20

Spirits Watching Over Me

In May of 2014, Elizabeth had an appointment in Kansas City, Missouri. She was planning to get up to take a shower early, so she could get there by 8 AM. I awoke about five, before the sun had risen, and decided to take a shower before she got up. I liked to take a shower in the early morning darkness, so I did not turn on a light.

I tried to open the shower door, but it was stuck. It came open a bit at the top, but it would not open at the bottom. I gave up the idea of a shower and figured I would go in the kitchen and make coffee instead. My plan was to sit in the living room and read the morning paper. I loved listening to the quiet of the early morning, and hearing the birds sing.

I walked out of the bathroom and, as I turned to go down the hall, a lightning bolt hit the cable wire outside my bathroom window. Electricity burst through the window inside the shower stall and hit the shower door. If I had been able to open the shower door, and turned on the water, I would have been toast. After that awful boom and crackle, I saw the shower door standing wide open. It had a brown spot on the Plexiglas, as if it was burned. Something like fine gold dust came down like a mist from the brown spot. When it hit the floor, it dissolved into nothing that I had ever seen before.

I will never be able to explain what it was, except that it was another gift. I thanked God and Mary again for saving my life. I guess I still had work to do for them.

59

21

Mary's Miracle to Me

My sister, Mary Grace, has always been interested in genealogy, always curious as to where our forefathers had come from. We knew a lot about our mother's family, but almost nothing about our father's side.

My father was forty-five years old by the time he married my mother. He had been married before, to his second cousin Brooke, and they had seven children together.

Five years after their divorce he met my mother who'd had female surgery. Her doctor told her that she would probably never have children. My father was very happy about that, since he had plans for them to travel around the world. It seemed that he could almost anything. He had been a motorcycle cop, detective, and railroad guard. He could sketch free hand, was an Interior decorator, a paper hanger, and a painter. Their plans were cut short because, within ten months of their marriage, Mother gave him a big surprise—a baby boy they named Carroll. After that, in rapid succession, came Margaret, Mary Grace, Lee, Mark, Joy, John, and then me, Gladys, surprise number eight. So much for my father's dreams of seeing the world. However, he still had the ambition travel, which accounts for the fact we were each born in a different state.

Recently, when DNA tests became available for the public at a reasonable price, my sister sent her swabs in to find out about her blood lineage and where we had our origin. The result was a double miracle.

61

My father's family was from Scandinavia. My mother's line was from the England, German, and Wales and Scotland, which we already knew. Tracing our genealogy, we found there was another line on my mother's side that came as a complete surprise—and, yet, before my sister even told me on the phone, I mentally already knew. It had been buried deep inside my memory bank. It rang a small bell in my mind, because I knew I had already heard this, but where? No one on this earth had known it before and, if I had told my family about it ahead of time, they would have laughed me out of town and dropped me in the ocean. The shocker for everyone else: I am, along, with my family, Jewish.

When I heard this, there was an echo in my mind, where all my life, came to pass. I had come full circle. I was in tune with my beloved Mary, the Mother of Jesus. I am blessed. Mary told me three things when I went up to Heaven, (1) I was of her family, (2) that I was of royal blood, and (3) that I would rule when I returned. This was too much for my earthly mind to understand, but when I return to my Heavenly home the answers will be revealed to me.

I possibly may be part of the Lost Jewish Tribes of Iraesl, Desporia, going back to Neo Assynin 722, BCE, in the land of Judea. The house of King David and the blood line of Mary, the mother to Jesus. I feel blessed.

There has to be some reason that Mary and I talked in the Garden and she told me these things. I am being taken care of by her, watched over and protected by her Heavenly Spirits. They are in their space and I am in mine, but they can come and go, I cannot, so I just wait.

Time is now coming for me to go and meet my God, and Mary, and see my beloved husband Warren at the gate. I feel, in writing these two books, that I have done what I was asked to do; to give people hope and to let everyone know that they are not forgotten, that their Spirits, sent from God, are with them every day. All you have to do is ask God to help you.

I am on full oxygen all the time, day and night, standing or sitting. My system is slowly shutting down. After all, I have led a long life, and it is my time to leave this world. I am excited about what is ahead of me. God is Great. *His love is endless.*

This world is in turmoil, but you must remember that God is with all of us; He is our Lord and Savior. Trust in Him and keep your faith, for He is close at hand.

22

My Son's Miracle

My son, Bill, was sitting in his living room rocker, waiting to go to church one Sunday morning, when he saw a shadow cross in front of him. It was two and one-half years since his dad had died, and he missed him. At first he thought it was just an illusion, or possibly a fine mist or dust particle passing before his eyes, until he heard a faint voice in his mind call his name. He hoped it was his dad letting him know that he was still with him. When Bill heard this soft whisper, he felt at peace.

As he was driving down the road, on his way to church, he noticed, out of the corner of his eyes, what he thought was a figure of a man sitting in the passenger side of his car. When he looked, the man smiled and waved like his dad would wave at him. Again the feeling of peace came over him. When he got to church, he got out of his car and looked again at the passenger side, but he could see no one there.

He went on into the church where a gentleman, unknown to Bill, asked if the man in Bill's car was coming to church as well. Bill looked back and saw a figure sitting in the passenger side. He knew that going out to get the man would not accomplish anything, so he told the gentleman who had asked the question, that his dad would come in when he was ready, and Bill went on into the chapel.

From that time on, it made a true believer out of him. God does a lot of exciting things to get your attention, and to help you remember that He is still alive and well.

23

Esther's Miracle

I am going to let Esther Luttrell tell, in her own words, about a miracle that involved me and my husband Warren.

**

Once a year, the Topeka & Shawnee County Library hosts an event that features dozens of Kansas writers. As a published author, I had participated for the past couple of years, leading up to this one event in the autumn of 2014.

The library doors open to the public mid-morning. From then until closing time we meet and greet readers that we hope will become buyers. At the end of the day, all of the writers are an exhausted lot.

It had been a good day, a lot of old friendships were renewed, a lot of new ones begun. It's not unusual for writers to exchange their work with colleagues, so I thought nothing of the nice-looking gentleman who approached me with a pleasant smile and outstretched hand, offering a slender copy of what he said was a book written by his wife.

I remember thinking *what a sweet man...* He had the countenance of someone who might have been a minister or a missionary, perhaps. His suit was very nice, well-cut,

67

conservative. Everything about him sent a signal that he was a good person, someone nice to know.

Still, I confess, I was tired and looking forward to packing up my display and going home to dinner. He didn't really have my full attention until he said, "My wife died and spent some time in Heaven..."

I was listening now.

Encouraged, he said in a soft, pleasant voice, "This book is her account of what happened while she was in Heaven, she's not a writer, but she felt like she had to tell the story. Our minister read it and gave an entire sermon on it, in fact, we've learned that ministers across the country have read her story and have devoted their service to her message."

"Really?" I said, turning the lovely little book over in my hand. The title was *You Live Forever*.

Before he left, he added, "My wife is at a table in the rotunda. If you have a chance, she'd like to meet you."

I thanked him and he went on his way. By the time I said goodbye to friends and got myself packed up to go, there was no one left in the rotunda, so I didn't get to meet his wife.

It was several months later, perhaps six or so, before I remembered the book. Curious, I picked it up and began to read. The gentleman—I confess I did not remember his name—was right: the author was no writer, but I felt it worked in her favor. She sounded like a plain woman, an honest woman who'd had a remarkable experience and truly didn't know how to tell about it except in her own simple words. I believed her.

I was concerned, though, because I found so many typographical errors that were the responsibility of the publisher, not the author. They detracted from the story.

Hoping I wouldn't offend Ms. Hargis, I looked her up in the phone book, called and asked if she would mind if I pointed out the most glaring mistakes, and then let me edit it for her, to be re-published, so that readership might be broadened. She had a message that the world needed to hear: Gladys Hargis had died in a hospital emergency room, was escorted to Heaven by an Angel where she met with other Angels and even had a conversation with Holy Mother Mary. She was eager as a child to let everyone know she had been given proof that life is eternal—after all, she saw her deceased parents. She also wanted everyone to know that God loves each and every one of His children, that we are given Spirits to watch over us, and that a beautiful life is waiting in Heaven for those who believe in Him.

Gladys took my offer to edit as graciously as she accepted life itself, and invited me to come to her house the following day.

Driving to her place, I recall thinking *I hope that pleasant gentleman is there. I'd love to see him again.* With that thought came a mental image of the man with the serene face and gentle eyes.

A woman, much taller than I expected, with a broad smile and a voice that certainly wasn't shy, greeted me at the door of her Topeka home. It didn't surprise me to learn that she had been raised on a farm. This was a plain-spoken woman without an ounce of pretense.

She sat in a big armchair, close to her supply of oxygen, while I perched on a footstool in front of her. As she went over the details of her amazing experience in Heaven, and what led up to it, I noticed a framed photograph of her husband on a shelf behind her.

Gladys had reached a place in her narrative where she asked an Angel if she might not be allowed to return to earth to help her ailing husband, Warren. The Angel conferred with other Angels. The consensus was that she could go back to care for him, but that she was "on borrowed time". Gladys wasn't dismayed to hear that; she was eager to return to Heaven—after helping Warren make his transition from earth to the Other Side.

I thought w*hat a fortunate woman to have two such grand husbands in her life,* for surely the man in the framed photo, the one I met, was her second husband. I said as much to Gladys. "Goodness, no," she protested. "I've only had one husband."

One husband? But she just told me Warren died. How could that be? The man in the photo was the man who handed me her book.

"Why, that's not possible," Gladys said. "He died more than a year before the library event."

We both looked at the inside of her book. The inscription read, "To Esther ... God Bless ... Gladys Hargis".

A man who died more than a year earlier had handed me a book that was inscribed to me—even though the author had never met, or even heard of, me.

Gladys, I realized, had been given a divine assignment: to see that her book was corrected and distributed to as wide an audience as possible, but I, too, had been given my own divine assignment: I was to help her get it done.

When Angels speak, it's wise to listen.

POEMS

by

Gladys Hargis
2016

Land Beyond the Veil / Gladys Hargis

The Golden Key called LOVE

I was blessed by the Spirit that was standing by my side,
He told me I was chosen to go back to being alive,

"Earth needs you more than ever" to spread around this love,
To let God's children know that He is still just up above.

He hears your cries, He is not deaf, He listens to us all,
He cares what makes you unhappy, He catches you when you
fall,

He's there for you, He always is, He says you must ask for
help,
He doesn't want to interfere you have to decide for yourself.

Don't ask for money, don't ask for riches, this will not buy
His love,
All He can do for you just now is give you plenty from
above.

Love is the answer to your living a very peaceful life,
Everything else just falls in place, as this is how you strive.

And when you find this thing called LOVE, GOD will know
you have found His key,
To life, and happiness, your dreams, and friends, your crying
will not be.

For He is there to take your hand and lift it to His breast,
Sometimes He checks with you to see if you have passed the
test.

And if you haven't found His key, this key that God calls
LOVE,   You will not enter Heaven's gate or be with us all
above.

And when your time on earth is done, and you join Him at the
throne
The blessed Spirit, sent by God, will see you are not alone

For He will be besides you, as He has from up above,
He will know that you have found the KEY, this golden Key
called LOVE.

Mary's Love

Mary is the mother of the Son of God today,
who died for sins we suffered all along the way.

I met her in the garden of Heaven's home up high,
She was sitting with her Angels, just below the bright blue sky.

She seemed happy to see me, as she set upon her throne.
She said that she had known me, from a long, long time ago.

She said that I was destined to see her in her chair,
to hear what she had wanted, for me to know and care.

When I returned to earth this time, I had a job from her
I was to let them know, that I was to insure.

That Heaven is a place set off for souls that needed rest.
And when they come into this Vale, they deserve the very best.

She said the world was getting awful, and something had to go,
That God had always been there ready, just for you to know.

Why did they not turn to Him, He could not understand,
when He could fix their problems, when they listened to His
plan.

He loved them so, He cared so much, to give them peace of
mind,
If just they loved their fellow men, and tried not to be unkind.

All they had to do was to give a little of their time,
to make the world a better place, so we all could live fine.

To love their neighbors as themselves, to share when troubles brew,
to balance out the strife's of life, and get ready for the new.

God is right beside you friends, He's all along the way,
all you have to do just now is bow your head and pray

And He will answer you in time, to solve the problems right,
Just give Him time to think it through, while keeping you in sight.

He wants what's best for you to have, to give you peace of need,
but not the money-grabbing things that you may want to heed.

For He will know what's best for you, what lasts for evermore,
and He will give you what you need, so just open up the door

And welcome in this Holy Man, who comes down from up above.
This key to heaven's gate has always been this word called LOVE.

Love Beyond the Light

God lights up His heavens, and darkness cannot be,
He has His own fuse box, called love for you and me.

He knows what you will need, every day of your life,
And when you get to Heaven, you will understand why.

He brought you into this world to do a job for Him
To live by His commandments, if you don't, the world will dim.

That is all that He has asked for, to love your fellow men,
To worship Him as your maker, to not commit any sin.

As long as His rules are followed, He will light up your way
And when it is time for you to come, He will send His angels to
say

"Come with me, friend of Jesus, come with me, it's time to go, I
have been sent from God to gather, from this place down below.

To a place where He has made for you, with beauty to behold.
Where loved ones who are waiting, way beyond the dark, dark
cold.

Where warmth of His lights are burning, for you to see your
way,
And He opens up your blessed life, just for you to say

'Thank you God for saving me from Hell's hot open door,
To take me into Paradise, where I will rise and soar.

77

And I will be with ones I hold dear, to never leave their side,
And never feel a threat or loss, to know that You will abide.

'For I've been searching all my life, to find You in the end,
And remember what You said to me, 'I will always be your
Friend'."

You've always been here by my side, but I would forget
sometimes,
Because I would feel the loss of You, especially when I was
unkind.

But now I am home, back in Your arms, to a place where I
adore,
And all I had to do to remember, was just open up the door.

In the Land Beyond the Veil

I awoke one morning beyond the dawn to find my body bound.
I felt GOD's hand upon my chest to say it was closing down.

The ambulance came and darkness took me off beyond their fold.
A presence was standing by my side to keep away the cold.

She led me up into a land where darkness cannot be.
Telling me to trust in her, and she would stand by me.

She sang in verse and melody that I would never die,
that I would live forever in the rooms up in the sky.

She said that GOD was waiting with all the angels by his   side,
to welcome me in glory and where I will reside.

Passing with her through the cleansing veil, I felt her nearness close.
I saw the city far away where I would be with those

Who had gone ahead of me and was standing at the gate,
to welcome me with opened arms to come and join their wait.

Smiles and happiness came from all, with open arms unfurled,
to bring me through the veil of life into their happy world.

I saw all my relatives, gone before, my parents, my siblings, and friends.
I saw Esther and Emma Ruth, my husband's mother and her kin.

I felt I had been here before in an earlier time in my life.
I felt I had just returned from earth, where there was so much strife.

I felt happiness overwhelm my soul, that gave out love to burst.
I knew I still had a job to do, but an earthly task came first.

I went back to get my husband, who would need my help for a while.
Then we both would return to glory, to the land up in the sky.

And I was assured that we would return to this land beyond the veil,
where we would reside forever where GOD would reign as well.

(written in 2010)

24

A Miracle from Warren

In August of last year, 2015, I was laying down for a short nap, when the telephone rang and a woman called and asked for me. She told me her name was Martha, but I was drowsy, and did not catch her last name. I asked her again, but it was hard to pronounce, so I just let her tell me what she wanted. She said she wanted to come and visit with me, and talk about my book I had written about my near death experience. I told her that would be okay, and we set the date for Friday. She then asked if my husband would be there, and I told her, "I am sorry, but my husband Warren passed away, November 24th 2012."

I could hear her draw in her breath and tell me that I must be mistaken on his death date or that I was confused about when Warren died. I politely told her that no, that is when he passed away. She became quiet and said she and her husband had visited with Warren the year before. That time was September 2014, when they had been at a book showing up north. I told her that was not possible.

I could hear her talking to another person and was checking with him about what she had heard me say. After that conversation ended with nothing cleared up, I told her that she was still invited to come and visit with me, and we would try to solve this mystery. She readily agreed, and she said she would like to bring her husband.

She called twice and canceled because things kept getting in the way, but finally she and her husband came down from a small town up north.

They were a very pleasant couple, and were very interested in my experience with ascending up into Heaven. I felt that the story I wrote seemed to take away any fears that they'd had about death of the body, and the ascending up to what God had in store for us. We talked for over two hours.

Her husband, Jake, told me that Warren was standing in front of the library at this small town of Wathena, and that he visited with Warren who told him, his wife, Gladys, had written a book called *You Live Forever,* about her dying experience, and being brought back from death. Jake said his wife was inside the library, and I am sure she will visit with your wife.

Martha, as I understood it, had lost a brother who, she was afraid, was not saved, nor did he want to be saved, as he did not believe in God all that much. This worried Martha a great deal. She wanted him to be with her in Paradise, and she had a lot of questions to ask me.

All I could say to her was to assure her that God has a way of making everything right. But I was sure that if someone had prayed for him, or if he was sorry at the last minute, he would probably meet her in Paradise. He might not be at the gate, but he would probably be forgiven sometime soon. I told her she needs to keep him in her prayers anyway, and God would hear her plea. I told her that if he murdered someone, now that might be a different question, as I hold murder and rape of children, at the top of the list of unforgiven.

They explained to me, and described to me, what Warren looked like, and how he seemed pleased about me writing a book. Martha said he had on expensive clothes, very high style, and silky. They both assumed that we were very well off. He looked like, and talked like, he had been well educated, and that we both had come from fine families. They said Warren beamed whenever he talked about me, as he was proud that I had lived to tell about my story.

My husband enjoyed visiting with them, and they walked on up to the town square to watch the people buying from the sidewalk sale. They said their goodbyes, and all three separated. When the problem came up about her brother, she and her husband decided to come to Topeka, and visit with me.

Martha and Jake were surprised to find that Warren had died two years before she and Jake had seen him. I told them not to mind about it because, with things happening as they did with me, I find God worked in mysterious ways, as He does with me—and my Angel gets a little frisky at times. Nothing surprises me anymore.

They both said they loved me, and said their goodbyes and left. I am sure they will come again sometime. There are mysteries around every corner, when it comes to God and he workings. The answers will come in his time.

THANK YOU, ESTHER LUTTRELL

I have an editor, a well-known mystery writer, Esther Luttrell, who helped me get this book ready for publication. Without her I don't know what I would have done. She is helping me keep things in order. This story repeats some of the information from my book *You Live Forever*, but I felt I had to put some things in to give this book a background.

I still needed that large handwriting on the wall, that I asked for when I returned from the land beyond the veil, to clearly tell me what to do, but with, my spirit and Esther, I think I have accomplished that for now.

My One and Two Book Store

This book reminds me of a man I met in Bisbee, Arizona, who wrote a book, called *One Book* about Him and his donkey Henry. He invited me over to his shop of books—which was called, ONE BOOK—and when I went in, I was expecting to see lots of books, so I could browse through the store, but instead all I found were many, many books of his *one* book. It sold so well, that after years of being pressured, he did finally write another book.

Well, this is all I am going to write: two Books. My store will be in Heaven, so come and browse with me.

Gladys L. Hargis,
2016

ABOUT THE AUTHOR

GLADYS HARGIS

Warren and I were married in Holton Kansas, July 31, 1949.

I graduated from Hoyt, High School, Hoyt, Kansas and continued my education in Business College. I was employed by the Santa Fe Railroad, while Warren joined the Topeka Fire Department.

I continued working until our son William was five months old. Then we took in day care children, finally foster children. We drove school buses part-time to help with our budget, so we could continue to help support all the children we had taken in to raise. In addition to William, I have three foster children, Joanie, Sandra, and Donnie; eight foster grandchildren, and four great grandchildren.

After Warren and I became empty nesters, we continued working for the State of Kansas, Warren as a fire and safety officer and I was a driver for the State of Kansas.. We finally retired for the last time.

Land Beyond the Veil / Gladys Hargis

BOOKS BY GLADYS HARGIS

YOU LIVE FOREVER, YOU LIVE FOREVER, YOU LIVE FOREVER

LAND BEYOND THE VEIL

Gladys Hargis books are available on Amazon in print, or may be ordered through any bookstore. They are also available as an eBook and may be purchased through Amazon/Kindle.

The author is always glad to hear from readers. Feel free to send her an email at ollieblack7@live.com.

Be A Book Angel

If your company or organization would like to provide
either, or both, of the author's work free to hospices
and bereavement groups, contact Gladys Hargis for
arrangements - ollieblack7@live.com

Made in the USA
Middletown, DE
08 February 2019